christian the lion

christian the lion

based on the amazing and heartwarming true story

ANTHONY BOURKE & JOHN RENDALL

Adapted for children by Ruth Knowles

delacorte press

Copyright © 2009 by Anthony Bourke and John Rendall

All rights reserved. Published in the United States by Delacorte Press,
an imprint of Random House Children's Books,
a division of Random House, Inc., New York.
Published in paperback in Great Britain by Red Fox,
an imprint of Random House Children's Books,
a division of The Random House Group Ltd, London.

Based on the story of Anthony Bourke and John
Rendall originally published as *A Lion Called Christian* in 1971.

This book is substantially a work of nonfiction based on the life,
experiences and recollections of Anthony Bourke and John Rendall.
In some cases the names of people, places, dates,
the sequences and details of events, and the actions and
conversations of real-life figures have been changed.

Delacorte Press is a registered trademark and the colophon
is a trademark of Random House, Inc.

Visit us on the Web! www.randomhouse.com/kids

Educators and librarians, for a variety of teaching tools, visit us at
www.randomhouse.com/teachers

Library of Congress Cataloging-in-Publication Data is available on request.
ISBN 978-0-385-73856-9 (trade) – ISBN 978-0-375-89562-3 (e-book)

The text of this book is set in 14-point Bembo.

Printed in the United States of America

10 9 8 7 6 5 4 3 2 1

First American Edition

To Christian and all animals
that enrich our lives

The four little cubs padded about, blinking in the sunshine and wrinkling their noses, making tiny mewing noises as they encountered all the new sounds and smells around them.

Their faces were covered in fluffy tawny fur, they were still wobbly on their feet and their paws seemed far too big for their little bodies. But safe in their mother's enclosure at the zoo, the cubs were free to explore their new world. Mum followed her babies around proudly, ready to help them if they tumbled. Her orangey-brown eyes twinkled with joy as she watched her children – three girls and a boy – running and capering around the cage.

One of them, the male cub, left the others and went back to the safety of his mother's side.

The beautiful lioness, Mary, lay on the ground, twitching her tail – flicking it up in the air and then down again. Her son watched, mesmerized, before pouncing and chewing it. After a while he grew tired of playing. He cuddled up to his mother and was soon asleep. His sisters joined him and settled down for a nap.

Their father, Butch, looked on from a distance, handsome and proud, with a large mane that was darker than his silky coat. It was hard to believe that the male cub, curled up next to his mother, would one day grow up to become a powerful and noble beast like his father, feared and respected by animals and humans alike.

But that was a long way off. For now, the new family lay snuggled up together, warm and safe and happy . . .

CHAPTER ONE

A few months and hundreds of miles away, shoppers bustled in and out of a grand London department store looking for last-minute Christmas presents. Carols rang out across Harrods' many floors and staircases; decorations adorned every surface and lights sparkled all around the building. People rushed around trying to find presents for their friends and families, eager to get home.

They weren't rushing past the exotic animal

department, though. A small crowd had gathered there. Children and adults alike were gaping at a cage, not quite able to believe their eyes. There was something wonderful inside . . .

Lion cubs! There were two, and they were the size of small dogs, with mottled, faintly spotted fur. One of them, the girl, looked angry. She pressed herself up against the bars of the cage, baring her teeth and snarling at the unwelcome attention. But her brother was different. Much calmer and quieter, he lay there, staring out past his enraptured audience. It seemed like he was focusing on something in the distance.

Despite the crowds that had gathered round the cage, two friends doing their Christmas shopping almost missed the cubs. Ace, the taller of the two, was fair, while John had long dark hair. They had just moved to London from Australia and were talking excitedly about the presents they planned to send back to their families. Strolling past the cage, chatting away, they completely failed to notice what was going on right beside them.

"I've no idea what to get for my mother," John moaned.

"Stop whining!" Ace told him. "Apparently you can buy *anything* in this store! We'll find something – don't panic."

"I hope—" John started.

But at that very moment, both men spotted the cubs, just metres away from them. They stopped dead in their tracks, their mouths dropping open in amazement.

"I don't believe it!" Ace exclaimed.

Awestruck, John shook his head. "Wow!" he whispered. "You really *can* buy anything in this shop!"

The lions were now playing what looked like a game of tag. They nibbled on each other's ears, then pounced, rolling around in a clumsy jumble of tawny fur. The two men moved closer, crouching down beside the bars and staring in wonder at the beautiful big cats in front of them.

Eventually Ace spoke. "It's so sad to see them locked up in this tiny cage." He frowned. "I bet they don't even know what Africa looks like."

John was angry too. "I can't believe it," he said. "That cage is *tiny*. I wish there was something we could do."

Ace was right. The cubs had never seen their African homeland. They had never lived in the wild with other animals. Born in a zoo in Devon, they had lived happily there for a while, but they had soon all been sold. This brother and sister had been bought by Harrods: at the age of nine weeks they had been separated from their parents and two other sisters and sent to live in London. At least in the zoo they'd had space to move around and explore; but it was obvious, as they wrestled playfully with each other, that something needed to be done about their cramped new home – and quickly.

Suddenly the male cub seemed to notice Ace and John watching him and stopped his game. Padding across to the bars of the cage, he fixed his beautiful rust-coloured eyes on each man in turn.

John and Ace gazed right back at him, hypnotized by the cub's huge eyes. Time seemed to stand still.

As the fluffy little lion continued to gaze at them, fascinated, John turned to Ace. "I—" he started. But then he stopped and shook his head. "No, it's silly – forget it."

Ace looked puzzled. "Forget what? Go on – what were you going to say?"

"It's just . . ." John paused again.

"What?!"

"Let's buy him."

"What? Really?!" Ace gasped.

Disturbed by the noise, the lion cub lifted a front paw and patted the side of the cage, making the bars rattle.

The two friends looked down at him again and smiled.

"Why not? I just can't bear the thought of him staying here," said John.

Ace looked at him, incredulous. But John held his gaze – he clearly meant what he'd said.

After a minute, realizing how determined his friend was, Ace agreed. "OK . . . Let's do it! Do you hear that, little fellow?" he asked the lion cub excitedly. "You're coming with us!"

The big cat's eyes were bright. He seemed to be listening to every word they were saying. He knew this was something exciting and was now gazing out at Ace and John, eager to see what would happen next.

Then, glancing around at the Christmas lights and decorations, Ace had an idea. He turned to John. "We should call him Christian," he suggested.

"Christian . . ." John mused. "I think I like it . . . *Christian*."

The cub lifted his head and seemed to nod at them. By now Ace's hand was gripping one of the bars of the cage. Christian stuck out his long tongue and licked it.

John grinned. "He likes it too!"

"Christian it is, then."

CHAPTER TWO

John and Ace hovered around near Christian's cage, nervous and excited at the same time. Fortunately they didn't have to wait long before Christian's keeper, Sandy, introduced herself and asked them if they needed any help. She was small and pretty, with brown hair and striking blue eyes. John quickly explained how keen they were to give the little cub a new home.

"Well, the female's already been sold — but, yes, this one's for sale," she told the two friends.

"I'll miss him terribly when he's gone – he's so gentle and affectionate." She paused and a smile crept over her face. "The staff across the way *will* be pleased, though! He may look cute and cuddly but he caused havoc in the carpet department last night!"

The picture of innocence until they'd made it past their keeper, Christian and his cheeky sister had escaped into the carpet section during their exercise time the previous evening. The cubs had enjoyed the feeling of freedom in this big open space and had played like naughty children amongst the beautiful, expensive rugs and throws. Running and tumbling around, they had explored every inch of their surroundings, just as they had at the zoo.

When she'd finally caught up with them, Sandy wasn't amused. Their little teeth and claws were very sharp, and the state of some of the carpets showed they hadn't learned to control them yet. She'd scooped up Christian and his sister and had carried them back to their cage, one under each arm. Glancing down at their playful faces, she couldn't stay cross for long. "You're adorable now, but I wouldn't like to upset you when you're all grown up!" she told them.

John and Ace looked at each other – were they making the right decision? they wondered. If Christian could run riot in a huge place like Harrods, what would he be like in their tiny flat? This was going to need some serious planning!

Meanwhile, Christian and his sister had recognized Sandy's voice: hoping that she'd brought them a treat, they'd moved closer to the bars and were trying to get her attention by patting her legs and meowing. They weren't disappointed. She threw a plastic ball into the cage, which Christian immediately swatted with his paw. Now, with the cubs distracted, Sandy started to tell John and Ace all about Christian's life. Unaware that his future was being decided just outside the cage, he and his sister happily chased after their new toy.

The next stage was for Christian to meet Ace and John properly so that he and his keepers could decide whether they would make the right human guardians for him. So, when Harrods finally closed for the day, John and Ace returned to Christian's cage in the animal department. They were feeling tense, and Christian appeared to be nervous too. For once he looked even more agitated than his sister: pacing the floor of the cage, he seemed to know that something important was about to happen. He had been a real attraction at Harrods, with lots of customers eager to have their photographs taken by his cage, but so far nobody had been serious about buying him. Would this time be any different . . . ?

While they waited, John and Ace talked quietly to each other. "I know Christian seems gentle and friendly, but, well, he is a *lion*," Ace whispered to his friend. And he was right. Christian was just like a cute, fluffy kitten now, but in a couple of years' time this tiny cub would grow up to be the king of the jungle.

John took a deep breath. "Yes," he replied, "but he wants to come with us – I just know it. And besides, we can't possibly leave him here, can we?"

Moments later Sandy opened the cage, and the little lions padded out. "Both cubs have been handled by humans since birth," she explained. "Christian really loves to play and be cuddled."

The female cub didn't seem to be interested in John and Ace; as soon as she smelled her evening meal – chunks of raw meat and a raw egg – she ignored them and started searching for her supper. But Christian was curious, and his jewel-like eyes inspected them closely.

The two friends had knelt down to be on his

level. As Christian approached, John reached out to stroke him. To his delight the little lion responded by clambering onto his knee and rubbing his forehead and face against his neck.

"What's he doing?" asked Ace softly.

"He's showing that he respects you," Sandy told them. "Whenever lions meet in the wild, they greet each other by rubbing their heads together like that."

Christian then moved from John's knee into Ace's open arms and solemnly repeated the ritual — the little cub had introduced himself. Sandy's face broke into a wide smile. "He likes you *both*," she decided.

CHAPTER THREE

The day Christian was to leave Harrods for ever arrived more quickly than seemed possible. When the time came, Sandy carried Christian to the shop's back entrance, where a car was waiting, driven by John's friend Joe.

The two friends from Australia shared a small flat on the King's Road above the furniture shop where they worked. They really wanted to give Christian a better home than the tiny cage he'd become accustomed to, so they knew they would have to move. They searched for days, looking for a big enough home with a garden for Christian to play in.

They just couldn't find anywhere that was quite right. But then they had an idea — it meant they wouldn't have to move after all: Christian could live in the big basement of the furniture shop! And they soon solved the problem of finding somewhere for him to run around: the nearby church had a big garden and the kind vicar told Ace and John that he'd be happy for them to exercise the lion cub there. So, with the basement cleared out and cleaned, and the freezer stocked with meat, Christian's new home was ready.

Now, as he was about to leave Harrods, Sandy held him close. He looked back at her with sadness in his eyes. As tears rolled down her face, he gently put his paws around her neck and licked them away.

She kissed him on his soft button nose.

"Goodbye, little man," she whispered quietly, carefully setting him down between Ace and John in the back of the car. He sat perfectly still.

"Don't worry, Christian. She'll come and visit you," Ace told the cub, stroking his head.

But Christian looked back at Sandy out of the rear window, saying a silent goodbye to the second mother he had known.

As soon as he was on his way to his new home, Christian's mood changed dramatically. He'd spent all of his young life behind bars, and this new world was very, *very* scary; he didn't know what to do with himself. His eyes darted around restlessly and he pawed at John's and Ace's faces, crawling all over them, desperately trying to find a way out of the car.

The two friends tried to distract the little cub. They gave him the big teddy bear they'd bought him as a welcome-home present, but Christian just wasn't interested. He patted the bear away with his paw before clambering around the car again.

Meanwhile John and Ace's friend Joe was struggling not to crash the car. He pulled over to the side of the road and stopped.

"Guys," he said frantically, "you'll have to calm him down or none of us are going to make it back to the shop alive."

Christian seemed calmer now that the car had stopped. John and Ace spoke gently to the frightened cub, patting and stroking him. Since their first meeting they had both been back to Harrods to play with Christian nearly every day, and the cub was beginning to get used to them. Having relaxed a little, he realized that he was with friends he could trust.

Miraculously, Christian stayed calm as the car started off again, and when they reached the shop he was happy to be carried inside and down to his new home.

In the basement he blinked, obviously a little overwhelmed and disorientated by his surroundings. But soon he was padding quietly around his new kingdom, sniffing every nook and cranny. John and Ace followed him nervously, just as his mother had done months earlier at the zoo.

The basement was perfect: even though it was below ground level, it was light and airy, with several rooms where Christian could prowl around and explore to his heart's content.

He inspected everything, checking out each and every cushion, toy and ball that Ace and John had brought for him to play with. His clever eyes didn't miss a thing.

The two friends watched Christian anxiously, desperate for him to be happy in his new home. John frowned. "Can we do this?" he asked Ace. "Can we really raise a *lion*?"

But it was Christian who decided to answer his question. He padded over to the two men and looked up at John – he wanted to play. He stretched up to place his paws on John's chest, then licked his face.

John gasped, delighted by Christian's show of affection.

"I think we can!" Ace whispered.

Christian was home.

CHAPTER FOUR

In just a few days Christian seemed to have settled into his new life with John and Ace, and it soon felt like he'd been with them for ever. Even during those first days the lion cub grew bigger and stronger than he'd been in Harrods. But even though he soon looked more grown up, Christian still loved to play, and from the moment he moved in he made sure that his new guardians knew it. If one of the men was talking to the other, or was on the telephone,

Christian would climb up onto his knee and pat him gently to show that he wanted some attention.

John and Ace had carried Christian's giant teddy bear downstairs into the basement, thinking he might like to play with it. But Christian had pulled it to pieces in just a few minutes, and bits of the teddy bear were soon to be found scattered around the basement rooms.

The cub quickly became brave enough to wander up the stairs and into the furniture shop; once there, he soon found much more interesting things to play with than a *teddy bear*.

On the afternoon of Christian's first full day with them, John and Ace got another shock when they went down to the basement: the little cub was running around with a waste-paper bin on his head! At first they thought he had somehow got himself stuck, but they soon realized their mistake. Christian was tossing his head about playfully, growling to himself. John and Ace removed the bin, putting it to one side of the room, but Christian chased after it and proceeded to tear it apart. The raffia strands soon joined the bits of teddy bear strewn across the floor!

On his second day in his new home, Christian was woken at eight o'clock.

"Good morning!" called John as he clattered down the stairs to the basement. To make sure that Christian would be as comfortable as possible with them, John and Ace had installed a heater in one of the basement rooms and placed a pile of blankets next to it so there would be a warm place for the little cub to sleep. It made a cosy bed, and Christian was reluctant to wake up. When John called out, his fuzzy face peeked out from the blankets, looking confused. He blinked sleepily before stirring and slowly getting to his feet.

John carried Christian over to the big

kitty-litter tray near his bed. The clever lion cub was already beginning to understand what it was for. Every time he made a mess on the floor, John and Ace carried him over to this tray.

"Well done, Christian!" John told him when he was finished. "We'll have this sorted in no time."

Ace soon joined them in the basement, carrying Christian's breakfast. Realizing what was coming, Christian woke up properly and careered over to Ace, almost knocking the meal out of his hands in his eagerness! In the mornings, and again just before he went to bed, Christian was given some vitamins and minerals with milk. But he much preferred his two other meals of the day! John and Ace brought him big chunks of raw meat from their favourite butcher and served them with a raw egg and some calcium, to make sure that his bones grew big and strong.

Christian still had a great deal of growing to

do. At the moment his head and paws looked much too big for the rest of him – his little body needed to put on a growth spurt to catch up.

Looking at the cub's huge helping of meat, Ace laughed. "I wouldn't mind eating that myself."

It did indeed look very tasty – it seemed far too much for such a small animal. But Christian always gobbled it down with relish.

After spending the morning playing, Christian prepared to visit his garden for the first time – the place that was to be his daily exercise ground from now on. He sat patiently as John and Ace put the specially made Harrods collar and lead around his neck. Somehow they made him look very little.

Remembering how scared the cub had been in the car when they drove home with him, they felt anxious about taking him into the outside world again. He'd been introduced to a lot of new places and people over the past forty-eight hours, and they were reluctant to cause him any more stress.

"Maybe we should leave it until he's a bit bigger," John suggested tentatively.

"No," Ace said firmly. "He needs his exercise. It would be cruel to keep him cooped up, and besides, we brought him here so that he could have a better life."

Christian pulled on his lead like an excited puppy. He agreed with Ace – he wanted to get outside!

CHAPTER FIVE

Leaving the shop, Christian padded happily onto the pavement. He ran ahead of John and Ace along the busy King's Road, straining at his lead. Pedestrians stopped and stared in amazement. Some came over to John, Ace and Christian, enthralled to see a real lion cub in London – they couldn't believe their eyes!

Suddenly it seemed like Christian became aware of all the activity around him. All the loud noises – voices, traffic, car horns and sirens – alarmed him and he started to panic.

Christian's eyes darted from side to side; then, without warning, he sat down in the middle of the pavement. Ace nearly tripped over him in surprise.

Very worried, John asked, "What's going on?"

"No idea," Ace replied. "But if we take it slowly, I'm sure the little guy'll be all right in a minute."

Ace was wrong. Crowds of people started to gather around Christian, frightening him even more. Crouching down beside him, John gently stroked the cub's head and back. For the next few minutes the two men tried to calm Christian down, but they soon realized that he wouldn't be persuaded to walk along the pavement any more. His little body was shivering with terror, his eyes wide with shock.

Finally, ignoring the crowd of onlookers, Ace scooped Christian up in his arms and, holding him close, quickly carried him the rest of the way to the church garden.

After the drama of his first visit, Christian grew to love his daily exercise. The garden was beautiful, and he felt safe there. Surrounded by a high brick wall, it had a big grassy area and lots of trees and hedges to hide and play in. His favourite game was chasing a football: he would scamper after it energetically, bouncing and wrestling with it for hours. Now that Christian was getting so much fresh air and exercise in the garden; now that he had more space, more love and more food than ever before, he was growing bigger and bolder every day.

Back at the shop, he became more confident, climbing happily up the basement stairs to see John and Ace whenever he felt like it. His favourite place of all was the front window of the shop. He would often stay there for hours, sometimes snoozing, sometimes gazing out at all the people bustling past as he had in his cage in Harrods.

John and Ace's furniture shop had the rather unusual name of Sophistocat. Perhaps that was why, when they saw a big cat in the window, most passers-by and customers simply assumed that it must be a toy to match the name of the shop. Imagine their surprise when they saw Christian suddenly twitch his tail or gracefully climb down from his window seat.

The little lion was gentle with everyone he met, and many of those who initially visited just to stare at him became firm friends. But the cub also had a cheeky sense of humour and liked to surprise people by creeping up behind them and making them jump.

One wet afternoon Christian was sitting in his favourite spot, intrigued by the raindrops trickling down the outside of the window. It had been a quiet day in the shop, with very few visitors, so the lion cub turned his head when the doorbell jangled and a customer came in.

Christian watched as John went over to speak to her. She was short and slim and wore a smart brown suit. Her hair was dark and flecked with grey.

"Do you need any help, madam?" John asked politely.

"Yes," she answered carefully. "I'd like to take a closer look at that beautiful pine table over there," and she pointed to the table in the centre of the shop floor. On her way over, she stumbled on something and John had to take her elbow to steady her. She bent over, picking up the object that had tripped her up, but when she saw what it was, she immediately dropped it with a loud shriek.

The offending article was one of the huge bones that John and Ace gave Christian to chew on in between meals. It was a good way for him to exercise his jaws and keep his teeth sharp.

It also had the added bonus of stopping him chewing on the furniture in the shop – which Ace had caught him doing several times!

"What on earth is that?" the woman cried, once she'd recovered from her initial shock. "It looks big enough to feed a lion!"

Christian saw his chance for a bit of fun. Slowly and carefully, he climbed down from his seat in the window. The soft pads of his feet made no sound as he slunk silently towards the customer.

John picked up the bone and put it out of sight. "Oh, gosh, I'm so sorry. I hope you're OK. Actually, you're absolutely right, we do have a lion – his name's Christian. He has a habit of leaving his old bones lying around once he's bored of gnawing on them."

The woman stared at John for a minute, puzzled; then, assuming he'd made a joke, she burst out laughing.

By now Christian was right next to her; he

sat down by her leg, staring up at her. His eyes were twinkling mischievously.

"No, really, madam," John said seriously. "Look, we do have . . ." And as he spoke he pointed down at the lion cub.

Christian didn't move a muscle.

The poor woman looked down slowly . . . She couldn't believe her eyes. Shrieking in alarm, she jumped behind the nearest piece of furniture, terrified. Even when John crouched down to give Christian a cuddle and prove how gentle and playful he was, she wouldn't move from her hiding place. Eventually, after a lot of reassurance from John – along with a sit-down and a cup of tea – she recovered from her shock.

Christian, realizing the fun was over, sloped off to find something more entertaining to play with.

The little lion was content. He adored his new

space and all the attention and love he was getting. And John and Ace were as happy as they had ever been. They'd been warned about the problems of welcoming a lion cub into their home, but for now life was fun.

However, Christian was growing up fast. He was already four months old, and things were about to get a lot more complicated.

CHAPTER SIX

One day Christian was relaxing in one of his favourite places – the landing halfway up the stairs that led from the shop to the flat above. He liked being up high, so he felt comfortable there – almost as comfortable as he did in the shop window. Up there, he could chew on the banister and watch John and Ace as they went about their business.

After a while Christian got bored of being by himself. His ears pricked up, listening out for his friends, and his eyes searched around for them. At last, hearing their voices, he climbed down the stairs and into the shop.

Padding in quietly, he saw that John and Ace were busy with one of their regular customers, so he wandered around the shop by himself, sniffing the new bits of furniture that had recently come in. In the middle of the floor was a beautiful new table, ready laid as if waiting for people to come and have dinner at it. Christian snuffled around the legs of the table, but then, wanting a better view, he jumped lightly up onto it. As he landed, the tabletop tipped. All the glasses and cutlery and plates and candles slid sideways and fell to the floor with an almighty *crash!*

John and Ace rushed over just in time to see Christian's confused little face looking up at them from the pile of smashed glass, crockery and tangled tablecloth. They stepped gingerly into the mess and picked him up. Ace held him on his knee while John checked the pads of his paws for shards of glass. Christian seemed unusually subdued.

"What happened, little guy? What happened?" asked Ace.

However, it didn't take long for Christian to recover from his shock, and within minutes he was padding down to the basement to start a new game. He soon turned his attention to the big mattress that now lay on the floor downstairs. He loved to drag it around and pounce on it.

As he left the shop, John and Ace watched him and realized that their little lion no longer moved like an awkward cub; they saw what a big change had taken place since he had come to live with them four months earlier. He was too big to move unnoticed between the pieces of furniture, and was becoming too heavy to climb on them – as this latest incident clearly proved. Christian was growing into an adult lion.

The bigger he grew, the more of a stir he caused amongst customers when he made his entrance into the shop. The regulars always greeted him warmly, sometimes bringing him a treat and always ready with a cuddle and a pat. But more and more often, new customers were genuinely alarmed by the big cat that lived in the furniture shop.

Even though they still had a gentle and loving relationship with Christian, John and Ace sensed that things couldn't go on like this for ever.

"It's not really fair on the customers," Ace said one morning as they watched Christian scampering around the garden. "We know he's as soft as a teddy bear, but other people don't, and we can't afford to put them off coming into the shop."

And so, having lived with John and Ace for several months, Christian began to spend more and more time in his basement rather than being free to roam around as he had done previously. By now he bore little resemblance to the small, kitten-like creature Ace and John had bought on their Christmas shopping trip to Harrods. He had grown very quickly, and the beginnings of a mane appeared around his head. Only his eyes remained the same – intelligent and trusting. But as the weeks passed and his activities were more and more restricted, those eyes began to look sad. Was he going to be cooped up more and more in this new home?

It was a quiet day in Sophistocat. John and Ace had let Christian out of the basement and he was wandering around quietly, when suddenly he spotted something on the floor of the shop. He went over to take a better look. It was long and fluffy, just like a tail, and he patted it, intrigued. Seeing that nobody was looking, Christian snatched it up in his teeth and rushed down into his basement.

When John and Ace followed him to rescue the object — it was a fur belt that had fallen off someone's coat — they found him running around with it in his mouth, making excited sucking noises.

Ace approached him to take the belt out of his mouth, but for the first time Christian disobeyed his human guardians. He did not want to give it back. He laid back his ears, his eyes flashed a warning and he showed the men his ferociously sharp teeth.

John and Ace jumped back in shock. What had happened to their playful, cheeky little cub? Christian let out a snarl that echoed around the room and the two men looked at each other in surprise.

"Let's just leave him with it," said John softly, "and get out of here till he calms down."

But Ace shook his head, moving slowly away from Christian and keeping his voice as normal as possible. "No, we can't let him see that we're frightened. Let's just stay here and see if he forgets about it."

Christian did. After about five minutes he grew tired of the fur belt and tossed it to one side. He wanted to play, and pounced enthusiastically on John, just as he always did.

In his playful nature, he was still very much like a cub, but John and Ace now realized they should never forget that Christian was a wild animal.

CHAPTER SEVEN

Because it was so unusual to see a lion wandering around in London, Christian had attracted a lot of attention since he came to live with John and Ace. He had visits from newspaper photographers, television reporters, and lots of interested people who just wanted to have a look at him.

Now that the lion tended to stay in the basement during the day, if somebody came into the shop really wanting to see him, John and Ace would lead them down the stairs and introduce them. So for Christian it was quite normal when, one day, his two friends came down the steps followed by a man and a woman he had never met before. Both strangers seemed very friendly. The lady was pretty, with blonde, shoulder-length hair; the man was dark-haired and had a bushy beard. Christian bounded over, patting John playfully with his paw and licking Ace's face with his long tongue.

But these visitors were no ordinary customers. They were famous actors – but since celebrities often came into the shop, this was not particularly unusual. Their names were Bill and Virginia, and what *was* unusual about them was that they were the stars of a very famous film called *Born Free*. In the film, they played a couple in Africa who adopt an orphaned lion cub called Elsa and raise her themselves. When she is a fully-grown lioness, they release her into the wild so that she can live a normal life and meet other lions.

When Bill and Virginia walked into the shop, John and Ace had both gasped in surprise.

Naturally they assumed that the famous couple had come to see Christian. But the actors had had no idea that Christian even lived at Sophistocat – they had just been looking for a table for their dining room!

The couple were very natural with him – after all, they were completely used to filming with lions. Christian soon rubbed heads with them, giving them the respect he had shown to John and Ace the day they bought him from Harrods.

Having met Christian, Bill and Virginia played with him for hours. John and Ace asked them lots of questions about lions and Bill and Virginia found out all about Christian.

When the couple finally got up to leave, Christian seemed reluctant to let them go. He kept pushing his ball over to Bill, as if to say, *More, please!*

"We'll be back soon," Bill promised. And Virginia bent down for one last cuddle.

In the days following Bill and Virginia's visit,

Christian seemed to need more and more fresh air and space. When he knew John and Ace were watching, he would squat over his kitty-litter tray – even if he didn't need to – in order to trick them into taking him outside. The church that owned Christian's garden had reluctantly said that he couldn't use it in the daytime any more: he was starting to frighten people now he'd grown so big. John and Ace could only take him there very early in the morning before anyone else was up, but Christian was finding the long days with nothing to do very hard.

"I'm really worried about him," John fretted one day as Christian hovered by his tray, impatiently scratching at it.

Ace agreed. "We need to start looking for somewhere else – a place that can give him everything he needs."

He and John looked sadly at each other, realizing that their months of fun with Christian would have to come to an end.

The lion sensed his friends were upset about something; he padded over, patting them gently one after the other, before climbing up, one big front paw on each of them, and giving them a big lion-sized hug.

John and Ace hugged him back. "I can't imagine life without him," John said, smiling.

But they would have to – and things would move forward much more quickly than they had imagined.

A few nights later, Christian was disturbed from his sleep by John and Ace racing down the stairs to his basement, cheering and whooping. The lion was confused by their excitement, but he was always ready to play, and shook himself awake before joining them. It wasn't long before the three friends were rolling around playfully together on the floor.

"You're going to be free, Christian! Free!" Ace cried.

Something very exciting had happened: Bill and Virginia had invited John and Ace for dinner. When they arrived, the two friends had been astonished to discover the real reason for their invitation.

"I think we can help you solve the problem of Christian's future," Bill had told them, smiling.

Born Free, the film that Bill and Virginia had starred in, had been based on a true story about a man called George Adamson and his wife, Joy. Bill and Virginia had become very good friends with George and Joy and saw them whenever they could. George was a top expert on lions, and he still worked with them every day; now he had a plan!

George was upset to hear about lions like little Christian, who were born in captivity and then spent their whole lives trapped in cages, without meeting any other lions or living free – lions are wild animals, after all. He wanted to free a group of lions in a country called Kenya in Africa and let them live together there, just as they were supposed to. George was living in Kenya and he hoped that Christian could be one of these lions.

"What do you think?" Virginia had asked after she and Bill had explained George's plan.

John and Ace did not have to think about their answer for long. They had seen Christian's bright eyes growing sadder and sadder over the past weeks. They knew that their little home would not be the best thing for him for much longer.

"You're going to get out of here!" John shouted now to the puzzled lion.

Why John and Ace had woken him up to play in the middle of the night, Christian had no idea, but he could tell they were excited about something.

"You're going to Kenya. To meet other lions!" cried Ace.

Christian was going to be free.

CHAPTER EIGHT

Once they had accepted George's offer, things moved fast. Christian's amazing journey from life at Sophistocat to the wild plains of Africa was going to be filmed: a television programme would be made of his experience. Some of the cameramen – along with the director – were going to visit Sophistocat and get started on the footage as soon as they could. They would be filming Christian inside the shop as well as in his garden, and the whole place was going to be closed to customers while they did so.

The day before the television crew arrived, Christian had been shut in his basement for hours. John and Ace wanted Sophistocat to look as smart as possible, so they had started giving the shop walls and floor a new coat of paint; Christian would only have got in the way if he'd been allowed to run around there.

The cub had spent the day pacing the floor of his basement rooms, occasionally wrestling with his mattress or playing with his ball. When Ace carried his lunch down to him, he had crawled onto his knee in an attempt to make him stay there and play.

But Ace had to get back to work. "Sorry, Christian," he said, giving him a quick pat before rushing back upstairs again.

By the time the paint on the floor of the shop had dried and John and Ace could finally let Christian out of his rooms downstairs, he was *very* bored and couldn't wait to escape.

As soon as John opened the door, Christian pounded up the stairs to the shop, wrinkling his nose at the peculiar smell of paint that filled the whole building. He was padding around the freshly painted black floor of the shop, when suddenly his paw brushed against an open tin and knocked it over. Paint splashed everywhere! Scared by the noise and the mess the paint made, Christian jumped backwards. Things got worse. The cub slipped in the paint, which made him even more confused and frightened. As he attempted to escape from it all, his big paws slid out from beneath him. Finally he got to his feet and dashed back down to the safety of his basement, leaving a trail of paw prints all the way across the shop floor. The spilled paint was white, but the floor was black – all John and Ace's hard work had been ruined.

But when they raced down the stairs to check that Christian was OK, the cross looks disappeared from their faces and they burst out laughing. The cub was covered from nose to tail in the brilliant white paint.

"You look like a snow leopard!" John laughed at him.

He and Ace fetched two big towels and some paint remover, and got ready to return Christian to his normal colour. But the little lion was starting to get used to the smell and the feel of the paint on his fur, and he remembered that he had been cooped up all day. Now he wanted to play.

John reached for a towel, but Christian pounced on it as if it was a game. The men managed to pull it out from underneath him, but as soon as John reached for it again, the cub jumped on it, pinning it to the ground and tugging it out of John's hand. He did this again and again before he finally recognized the cross tone in John's voice; then he sat quietly with a hurt look in his eyes while they set to work on his beautiful caramel-coloured fur again.

Christian looked absolutely stunning when he was filmed the following day. His coat and eyes shone brightly; he moved gracefully and powerfully. He was so gentle and patient with the film crew that they had all fallen in love with him by the time the first scene had been shot.

Except for the one incident when Christian had run off with the fur belt, he had never shown a vicious or aggressive side to John or Ace, or any of his friends and visitors. He was as trusting and playful as he had been when he was a tiny cub, and he still seemed happy at Sophistocat.

The lion carried on with his tame house-trained life for a few weeks after the filming in the shop was finished. But plans for his future were already under way.

Bill and Virginia, Christian's new friends, had

been visiting him regularly and could see that he was beginning to feel frustrated. They were desperate to help him. Their garden out in the countryside was very large, so they decided to build a special area behind their house where Christian could stay until he was ready to go to Africa. Besides preparing for life there, he could escape the restrictions of the city and live outside with more freedom and space. John and Ace were going to move to Bill and Virginia's too – they would live in a caravan near Christian.

There were lots of things that Christian would need to know before he could travel to Africa – things that cubs born in the wild would have already learned by following and copying their parents. Christian was big for his age, but he had no experience at all of the challenges that lions in the wild face every day – having to hunt for food, or facing battles. Everything he needed had been handed to him by John and Ace whenever he wanted it. Hunting for food is dangerous, and Christian didn't even have the skills to hunt a rabbit.

"Can Christian survive life as a *real* lion?" asked a worried John one day as he played with the cub.

But he and Ace knew that they could not keep Christian cooped up with them simply because it would make his life longer and safer. It would be a pointless, boring life, and Christian deserved the chance to live with other lions.

Bill and Virginia were soon ready for Christian, John and Ace to move in. After spending five very happy months at Sophistocat, it was time for the cub to leave London for good and begin the first step of his journey to Africa.

CHAPTER NINE

Christian looked strong and powerful as he charged across the huge garden that was his new home. He loved the space and padded around happily, investigating every bit of it. He was like an excited puppy, stopping to sniff whenever he smelled something unusual before rushing off to look at something else.

Bill and Virginia had made the cub a wonderful enclosure: it was surrounded by a very tall wire fence so that he couldn't escape and would be completely safe. The large grassy area had a huge tree in the centre; there were bushes to play in and a brightly coloured caravan where Christian would sleep until he was ready to stay outside.

Every so often he padded back over to John and Ace, who were standing by, watching. He would run around them excitedly before leaping up at them. His eyes were bright and he licked their faces with his scratchy tongue, as if saying thank you for bringing him to this fantastic new place.

"Do you like it, Christian?" asked Ace cheerfully.

In response, the lion raced off around the garden again, stopping only to examine a daffodil before crashing straight through a patch of pretty blue flowers. It certainly *looked* as though he liked it! He clambered up the thick trunk of the tree and out onto one of the high branches. With his back to John and Ace,

Butch and Mary, Christian's parents,
at Ilfracombe Zoo, in Devon.

Christian didn't take to cars immediately, but soon grew to like looking around and seeing what everyone was up to.

Christian explored everywhere in the flat,
even the bathroom!

Christian
loved to sit
and play on
the stairs,
watching
everyone
below.

What's in here?

Photo © Derek Cattani

Christian loved to play in the church garden.

Christian met many celebrities — above with James Hunt, the famous racing car driver, and below with a well-known radio journalist.

Photo © Derek Cattani

Although Christian loved his home in London,
John and Ace knew it couldn't last forever.

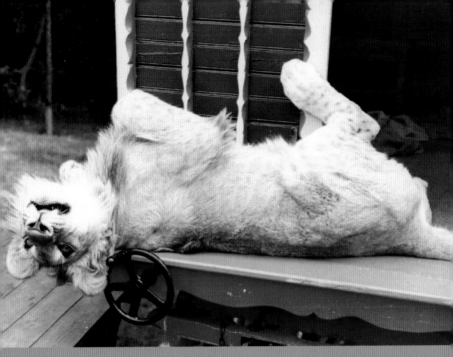

Here's Christian in the caravan and below with his good friends John and Ace.

Christian enjoyed playing in his new space.

Whoops! Where's he gone? We've lost a lion.

Ah, there he is!

Christian was growing up fast – his mane had become darker and thicker.

The journey to Africa was a bit cramped. Christian couldn't wait to get out and make new friends.

Exhausted after his long journey, Christian fell asleep
straight away when the party reached camp.

Christian's first walk on African soil.
Ace, John and George Adamson follow along behind.

George Adamson and Boy, the first male lion Christian met in Africa, and below with his little friend Katania.

One of John and Ace's last days with Christian.

Christian inspected his garden from on high, just as he had once surveyed the furniture shop.

After a while Christian realized that this branch was not wide enough for him to turn round on. He moved one of his paws gingerly and set it down in a different place, but the branch wobbled and he moved it straight back again – he couldn't get down!

John and Ace waited, watching him carefully, finally realizing that he couldn't work out how to get off the branch. Although he loved climbing, the cub was only used to jumping up onto the furniture at Sophistocat – tables and chairs that were at most a couple of metres off the ground.

The two friends rushed over. "Come on, Christian! Come down," Ace shouted encouragingly.

John joined in: "You can do it, Christian!"

Eventually they managed to coax him down, but he was confused and trembling when he reached the ground again. It looked as if they had been right to worry – he still had a lot of very simple things to learn.

Christian soon got used to life in the country. His life was becoming better and better: he was very happy.

One day, after living in his new home for several weeks, Christian came over to greet Ace and John as he did every morning. He jumped up and licked John's face first.

"Ow!" shrieked John, pushing Christian firmly away from him. He held his hand up to his face.

The lion looked hurt. He couldn't understand why John had seemingly rejected him, and he turned to Ace for comfort, winding himself round the backs of his legs.

Ace was confused too. "What's wrong?" he asked his friend.

John shrugged. "I don't know – it really

hurt." When he showed Ace his face, there was a big red mark where Christian had just licked him.

Christian was spending more time cleaning himself now that he lived outside, and his tongue was rougher than it had been – almost like sandpaper. When he'd licked John's face it had almost made him bleed.

There were lots of other similar changes in Christian. Running around outside all day, the cub was getting lots of fresh air and exercise. He was eating more too, so he grew bigger very quickly. Bill filled a sack with sand till it was very heavy, then tied it to the tree in the middle of Christian's enclosure. The lion loved to pounce on it and attack it. He also had a new heavy rubber tyre to roll around with, and playing with these toys soon started to make him more athletic and muscular.

Christian now looked beautiful, contented and healthy. His fur grew thicker and softer;

the colour had changed to a soft caramel. His mane was becoming darker and thicker too – the cub suddenly looked like a lion.

On a lovely hot and sunny day in the middle of August, John and Ace joined Christian to celebrate his first birthday. As they reached his enclosure, they were shocked to find that he had managed to climb nearly all the way up the wire fence. They gasped in surprise and rushed straight over. Christian clambered back down as soon as he saw them and came to say hello, just as he always did, but John and Ace were worried.

"Maybe he just wanted our attention," John suggested.

Ace shook his head. Christian was happy here – it was definitely better than Harrods or Sophistocat – but he was still being kept in captivity. Living here was like being in a zoo similar to the one his mother and father still lived in. All his life Christian had been behind bars; now that he had experienced a little bit of freedom, he wanted more.

That afternoon, as John and Ace gathered together – along with some friends from London – to sing "Happy Birthday" to Christian, they placed a meat-cake, with one candle on top, in front of him. Both of them made a wish: *Please let us get Christian to Kenya soon.*

And it looked as if Christian was wishing exactly the same thing . . .

CHAPTER TEN

It was a very long way from England to Kenya. When Christian finally set off on his journey to live with George in Africa, it would take him fifteen hours to get there. For this trip he wouldn't be able to travel sitting in between John and Ace as he had on the car journey from Harrods to Sophistocat. He would have to be shut up in a big wooden crate in a special part of the plane.

The crate was delivered to Bill and Virginia's

well in advance so that Christian could spend some time in it before he needed to use it for the actual journey. That way, they hoped, he would get used to it. When he caught sight of the crate, he sniffed around it for a long time before going inside. At first he simply walked in as far as he could go, then quickly backed out again. He didn't seem to like it very much. But over the next few days he agreed to eat his meals in it; eventually he even slept there. It *was* big enough for him to turn round and sit up in, but it was still a very small space in which to spend fifteen hours.

"I feel so bad," Ace said one day, a week or so after Christian's birthday. "How will he ever cope with being in there for such a long time?"

He and John were about to find out.

The very next day, Bill had a call from George in Kenya. George had been busy making preparations for Christian's arrival, and now everything was ready.

Bill came racing over to Christian's enclosure, whooping and cheering. John, Ace and Christian looked at him expectantly.

"Well?"

Bill grinned excitedly and grabbed Christian's paws. "You're going, fellow!" he said.

The young lion's eyes lit up, and he ran from Bill to John to Ace and back again, nudging them all. It was as if he understood the good news perfectly – he was going to Kenya!

Two days later, Christian went into his crate – this time not just for a few minutes, but for the entire journey to Africa, his final home. He climbed in and lay down, looking out at John and Ace, fixing them intensely with his amber eyes as the front was nailed up. The cub had been given some medicine to help him sleep during the trip, so he looked a bit dazed and he kept blinking. John and Ace stroked his paws. He seemed very calm, but they were worried.

"I know this is for the best," said John, catching a final glimpse of the sleepy lion as the crate was loaded onto the van that would take him to the airport, "but it's a really long way." John and Ace were going to fly to Africa on the same plane as Christian, but they wouldn't be able to see or stroke him until they arrived in Kenya.

"Christian's tough," replied Ace. "And he wants to meet the other lions in Africa. He'll make it."

And he did. But when Christian was finally unloaded from the plane and the door of his crate was opened, he was no longer relaxed and sleepy. The long journey in such a tiny space had been scary, and he was very agitated, but he padded out into this strange, hot country and headed straight for John and Ace. He pawed and cuddled them as if they had been apart for weeks, not just hours. He was still a little wobbly and looked very tired and somehow thinner. His coat seemed to have lost some of its shine and his eyes were still glazed.

John and Ace knew there and then that they had made the right decision in bringing Christian to Kenya. He looked dreadful just from having been cooped up in his crate for a day. They couldn't keep him trapped in a zoo or a house for the rest of his life, even if they were bigger than the box he had travelled in. Christian was going to be given space and freedom and a life in the wild.

For two days Christian stayed in a big enclosure at the airport, so that he could recover from his long journey before setting off again. John and Ace spent a lot of time with him there, and soon he was back to normal, wanting to play football with them despite the heat.

When he first met George, the man who was going to give him his freedom, Christian was his normal friendly self.

"He's a handsome little fellow, isn't he?" George said as Christian nuzzled his neck.

George had set up a camp for them to stay in for a few days before travelling on through Kenya to their final destination. He explained the plans to Christian as though the cub could understand every word of what he was saying.

For the journey to the camp, George drove the car, while Christian sat between John and Ace on the back seat, exactly as he had on his journey from Harrods.

There was a wire barrier between the back seats and the front seats of the car, and Christian kept rubbing his head against it, jerking from side to side agitatedly. It was very hot in the car — even hotter than it was outside. John and Ace became quite worried, and asked George to pull over so they could give Christian some water and try to calm him down.

Christian gratefully lapped up the water Ace

held out to him in a big bowl. He began to relax now that the vehicle had stopped.

John stroked his head as he drank, but suddenly Christian flinched away as if in pain. When John took a closer look at his head, he gasped in shock. Where Christian had been rubbing it against the wire divider in the car, there was some fur missing, and the skin underneath looked red and sore. There was a bald patch on his nose too. Poor Christian just wanted the journey to end, and to get out into the wild. He was finding this long hot journey very difficult.

When the car finally came to a stop at the camp, John and Ace looked around, eager to explore. But for once Christian was too tired to take in his new surroundings. He followed John and Ace slowly into the camp, jumped straight onto one of the camp beds and immediately fell fast asleep.

CHAPTER ELEVEN

When Christian woke the next morning, he looked around at the strange new country he'd come to. There was none of the green grass he had got used to in his garden near Sophistocat and in Bill and Virginia's enclosure. It was boiling hot, and everywhere was bare and sandy – exactly the same colour as Christian's fur. He blended into his surroundings perfectly.

He waited impatiently for John, Ace and George to wake; as soon as they were up, he wandered off a little way before coming back and nudging them with his nose. Christian wanted to explore!

Finally Ace and John were ready too. They took off the collar that Christian had worn every day since his first visit to the garden in London – it all seemed so far away now; he was no longer under their control. With John, Ace and George following, Christian set off on his first walk in the wild.

It was very hot, and the three men were sweating, but Christian strolled along happily, taking in everything around him. He seemed to feel freer without his collar; he certainly looked it, proudly turning his head from side to side as he surveyed the barren landscape.

Suddenly he paused for a moment, pulling up sharply and wrinkling his nose as if in pain. John and Ace looked worried and were about to run over to see what was wrong, but George stopped them.

"Look," he told them. "Wait."

Christian had managed to get a thorn stuck in his pad. He lifted his paw up to his mouth and started to work the thorn out with his teeth before licking the sore patch with his tongue. He knew, without ever having been shown or told, how to remove the thorn himself.

The men smiled, wondering if he would be able to tackle every problem as easily.

But there were much bigger challenges in store for Christian. Later that afternoon, he was near the camp when, without warning, he broke away from his guardians. He stood perfectly still, his ears back, staring into the distance.

"What's happening?" whispered Ace, concerned.

They soon had their answer. A huge brown and white African cow with big sharp horns wandered towards the camp. Searching for food or water, it had become separated from the rest of the herd. Christian began to stalk the large animal, creeping up on it from behind.

"We have to stop him!" George muttered softly to John and Ace. "He could get hurt!"

Christian had never hunted in his life – he didn't have the experience to do it successfully and could be seriously injured if he attacked the big cow and something went wrong.

The three men were very worried, but Christian seemed totally in control of the situation. He continued to pad softly around the cow, using the bushes as cover. He had positioned himself downwind of her so that she wouldn't pick up his scent.

Even though Christian was doing exactly the right thing, George was still nervous. Something could easily go wrong. He jumped into his car and drove in between Christian and the cow, separating them.

The cow was scared and ran off, but Christian's eyes narrowed and his ears flattened: he made to go after the animal. It was as though his natural instincts had kicked in: now that he had spotted his prey, he wanted to catch it!

John and Ace managed to grab Christian and hold him back. Half dragging, half carrying him, they tried to lift him back into George's car. When he was a cub they would have been able to do this easily, but now Christian was bigger and heavier, and it was struggle.

He was also formidable. For only the second time in his life, he snarled viciously at John and Ace, showing his sharp teeth. They were forced to let go of him and jumped back, surprised. Christian bounded off after the cow, leaving John, Ace and George in a state of shock.

Christian soon realized that the cow was long gone – he wasn't going to catch her – but he was still tense and on the lookout when he returned. He was angry with his friends for scaring away his prey, and at first he refused to follow them back to the camp, but after a last tour of the area, he finally padded along behind them.

George was impressed with how well Christian was adjusting to life in Africa and how naturally he seemed to behave in the wild. They moved on to a different camp closer to the place where Ace and John would eventually leave the lion for good with the rest of his new pride. It was a beautiful spot, surrounded by bushes and greenery and skirted by a large river.

Christian was not yet used to the heat in Africa – he didn't like it much, only venturing out in the early morning or late afternoon when it was slightly cooler – but he loved everything else about it. At first the pads on his paws were rubbed raw by the rough terrain. But soon, just like the rest of him, they began to change to suit his new surroundings. Every day he grew in confidence, and would now push his way ahead of John and Ace when they explored the area around the camp.

He no longer *needed* the men who had taken care of him, but he loved them just the same and would still demand hugs, sometimes knocking them to the ground now that he was so big and strong.

Only one thing remained to make his happiness complete. George would be releasing two other lions into the wild at the same time as Christian. Now that Christian had settled well here in Kenya, he decided it was time to go and fetch them.

Christian was going to make some friends.

CHAPTER TWELVE

Christian would be released into the wild as soon as possible, but over the next two years George planned to stay close to him and the other lions he was introducing to Africa. He hoped that by the end of this time all the lions would have formed a pride – a family – that hunted and got on well. Then he would be able to leave them completely on their own to live together naturally.

But there was no guarantee that Christian

would take to the other lions George was fetching, or that they would like him. He would need to be introduced to them slowly, over a period of some weeks, so that they could all get used to each other.

At first Christian would be separated from the other two lions by a tall strong wire fence. That way they would see each other every day before they were actually allowed to have any direct contact.

Finally the big moment came: John and Ace led Christian over to meet the other lions, and the cub from London caught his first sight of them. And what a sight it was!

The two lions were very different, both from each other and from Christian. One of them, the girl, whose name was Katania, was tiny. She was just four months old, and had been found alone in some bushes. George assumed that her mother was dead, so he had taken her in and looked after her. She was pretty and timid, with mesmerizing eyes and lovely long whiskers.

Christian hardly gave Katania a glance. His attention was drawn immediately to the other lion George had brought to their camp. John and Ace were impressed too.

"Wow!" whispered John.

The big lion was called Boy, and he was seven years old. Boy had appeared in the film *Born Free* with Bill and Virginia; at that time he had been fit and healthy and friendly. Some time later, George and his wife, Joy, had come across the lion on one of their walks and had recognized him immediately as Boy. He had been very badly hurt, and could barely walk, so they had taken him straight to a vet. He had undergone a very long operation: a steel pin had been put in one of his legs to help him walk again.

Now there was no sign that he was anything other than a fit, healthy, strong lion – other than a slight limp. Boy was a formidable creature, with a thick dark mane that made him look even bigger than he actually was. He stood there, fixing the young lion with an intense stare.

Christian tensed immediately. His fur bristled and his ears pressed back against his head. He was confused and frightened – too frightened to look directly back at Boy; he kept his head lowered, his eyes darting about nervously.

Christian noticed John and Ace starting to move towards George. The cub was reluctant to be left alone under Boy's gaze, so he quickly padded after them, pressing himself up against their legs.

Suddenly, with a terrible roar, Boy charged. The fence was in the way, so he couldn't actually reach Christian, but the wire bent and shook alarmingly. Luckily the huge lion didn't try to climb the fence to reach Christian; he simply took one last look at the cub before strolling away. Bravely, Christian stood his ground: though he still refused to look directly at Boy, he stayed exactly where he was on the other side of the fence, trembling and snarling in fear.

Christian was stunned. Until now he had believed he was the only lion in the world. And in his world, he *had* been. Other than his parents and siblings, whom he barely remembered now, he had never met another lion, and this first experience had not been a good one. Boy had done what every adult lion would do, demanding respect from him. He wanted to show Christian that he was in charge.

"Can't we take him away?" Ace asked, feeling sorry for Christian.

But George knew that Christian would have to get used to Boy if they were to form a pride; he shook his head, and they remained by the fence for half an hour, forcing the cub to stay close to the big lion.

Boy could see that he had scared Christian, and he seemed to be enjoying it. Every so often he would charge at the young lion, making him shake with fear and return to his hiding place behind John's or Ace's legs, where he would crouch down and pretend to be asleep.

Christian was *very* relieved when they finally led him away from the fence – away from the terrifying lion on the other side of it. He was nervous for the rest of the day, and followed John and Ace around closely, constantly checking that Boy was still safely behind the fence.

That night, still reluctant to leave their side, Christian slept on a bed between John and Ace. All three of them were woken in the night by Boy's powerful, haunting roars. He wanted Christian to know that he was still out there, and still in charge.

The next morning John and Ace were still worried about Christian. He stayed close by their side all the time and wouldn't concentrate when they tried to distract him with games. Every so often he would glance over at Boy and Katania.

"He just wants to lie on his bed all the time," John told George.

Having come all this way, would Christian be unable to settle with the other lions after all?

CHAPTER THIRTEEN

Later that afternoon, Christian took a brave step. He padded up to the fence that separated him from the other two lions. Boy kept his distance at first, but Katania came over almost immediately. She lifted one of her front paws to pat Christian through the fence; she seemed friendly. When Christian moved along the fence a little way, Katania followed him. She was definitely trying to make friends.

Christian and Katania were pacing up and

down beside each other, making happy little grunting noises, when suddenly Katania stood on her hind legs and put her front paws against the fence to try and get closer to Christian. This angered Boy, and he bounded over, charging at the wire again and interrupting the cubs' game.

Katania knew Boy well, but she was still terrified of him, and ran off immediately to hide behind a rock. Christian jumped, just as he had done the day before, and cowered away again. But instead of running straight back to John and Ace, he padded slowly over to them. He was shaking, and clearly still scared, but he had taken the first step in getting to know Boy.

Seeing that Christian and Katania wanted to be friends, George made a little hole, low down in the fence, big enough for Katania to crawl through. This meant she could choose whether to be on Boy's side or Christian's side. The gap was much too small for the big lion to get through, so Christian was totally safe from him. All the same, he wasn't ready to face Boy again yet, and he stayed near to John and Ace, pretending the other lions simply weren't there. It was as though Christian could not quite decide whether he wanted to be friends with them or not.

It looked like Katania couldn't decide either. Most of the time she stayed near Boy, only venturing over towards Christian's side when he wasn't actually there.

The next day Christian finally made up his mind about the other lions. He was stretched out on the ground in between John and Ace, one eye on the other side of the fence, where Boy and Katania were snoozing. All of a sudden he seemed bored of being with the humans. He strode boldly up to the fence and lay down just in front of it. Boy charged towards him immediately. Christian scampered away – he couldn't help it: Boy was just so huge. He hid behind John's and Ace's legs before returning to lie in front of the fence again.

"What *is* he doing?" wondered John.

Christian looked determined now, and was focused on Boy, watching his every move. The pair went through the same ritual several times. Boy would charge at Christian, chasing him away. But then the young cub would go back and lie in front of the fence again. He was teasing Boy – and it was working: the big lion was getting irritated with him. Boy nudged the wire with his proud head and prodded it impatiently with one of his paws.

"Cheeky little devil!" laughed Ace, shaking his head.

But although they laughed, John and Ace *were* concerned that Christian had become too confident too quickly. He suddenly decided he wanted to tease Boy even further, and stuck his head through the Katania-sized gap in the fence to look around. As soon as he saw

Boy approaching, he withdrew his head and lay down again. Boy was furious at Christian's impudence, and the fence shook as he rammed his body against it.

John and Ace had no idea why Christian was putting himself through this, but George thought it was important that he learn how to deal with Boy on his own. Finally, it seemed, he wanted some attention from his fellow lions.

The next afternoon George decided it was time for Christian to meet Katania properly. Boy was led out of his enclosure and Christian was led in, leaving him and Katania alone together.

At first Katania looked upset at being separated from Boy; he had taken care of her like the parent she'd lost. She paced up and down nervously, looking around for the bigger lion, sniffing hard to try and discover where he had gone.

But Christian was more confident now that

Boy had gone; he padded over to the timid little lioness. Standing perfectly still, he stared at her intently for a while. Then, slowly and deliberately, he leaned forward to rub his head against Katania's forehead and neck. Immediately she seemed to relax, and she did the same to him – the cubs had now introduced themselves properly.

Christian was fascinated by the young lioness. This was the first time since leaving his sister that he had been close to another lion. He licked Katania's face and sniffed her, getting used to her scent.

As he continued to lick her with his long rough tongue, there was a sudden commotion. From the other side of the fence, Boy charged again as if trying to stop Christian from making friends with Katania. But this time the impact was nowhere near as forceful as it had been before, and the wire barely rattled. He soon sat down again at George's feet. Was Boy starting to accept Christian? George wondered.

Christian and Katania paid no attention to the big lion watching them jealously from the other side of the fence. They played together as if they had known each other all their lives. Christian was bigger than the little lioness, but he was very gentle with her. She would scamper off, glancing back at him playfully; he would follow her and trip her up and, in a cloud of dust, they would roll around together like two little kittens. Christian had finally made friends with another lion.

CHAPTER FOURTEEN

Christian still faced the much bigger challenge of making friends with Boy. The next day it was their turn to be properly introduced.

John, Ace and George waited anxiously as the three lions were led out of their enclosures. If Christian and Boy got into a fight, the younger lion would stand no chance at all. He was far smaller and very inexperienced.

Christian had shown that he instinctively knew how to handle some situations – all the men could do now was hope that he would know how to handle Boy too.

"Fingers crossed," Ace whispered. It was a tense wait . . .

Minutes passed, but nothing happened . . . Boy, Katania and Christian all stood there, staring at each other. Christian did not approach the others: he seemed to know that, as the older lion, Boy would want to make the first move. However, Katania didn't have the instincts that Christian did and she suddenly got bored with the situation. She got up and wandered over to her new friend, greeting him enthusiastically and rubbing her head against his neck. Christian licked her face affectionately.

It was absolutely the wrong thing to do.

"Oh, no!" hissed John.

Boy stood up: he had never looked scarier as he proudly showed off his huge body and mane; then, with a terrifying roar, he charged at Christian . . .

Christian roared too, though his roar was drowned out by Boy's. John and Ace had their heads in their hands.

"Is he OK? Is he hurt?!" cried John.

Boy had pounced on Christian, pinning him to the ground, but the cub was unhurt. He rolled over on his back to show Boy that he had won. This seemed to please the big lion, and he strutted proudly back to his starting position.

Katania had fled in fright and hidden behind a rock, but a few minutes later she emerged, and approached Christian again. Exactly the same thing happened. As soon as Christian touched Katania, Boy charged at him, pinning him down. This time it took slightly longer for Christian to roll over in defeat, and when Boy eventually climbed off him, the young lion was shaking all over. He was *terrified* – he looked defeated and miserable, almost ashamed of himself, and, head down, slunk slowly towards John and Ace.

Christian seemed to have had enough of other lions for one day, and as he reached his old friends he rubbed up against them for warmth and comfort. They stroked him and talked gently to him just as they had when he was a young cub. But they were proud of him. He had now faced his first adult lion: he had not run away, but had confronted the much bigger creature head-on; and he had done the right thing in allowing Boy to win. Once again, Christian had shown that he instinctively knew how to behave like a lion in the wild.

However, after a couple of hours of being comforted by John and Ace, Christian decided he was not going to be put off by Boy: he picked himself up and approached the older lion again, determined to be accepted.

As Boy moved around, Christian followed him, doing exactly as he did. He sat when Boy sat, and lay down when Boy lay down. He did everything he could to make Boy like him.

The next day Christian seemed to be limping. Worried that Boy had attacked him when they hadn't been watching, John and Ace beckoned to him. But when he ran over to his friends, Christian was moving normally – his limp had suddenly gone.

The men were puzzled. They inspected Christian's paws, but there were no thorns stuck in his pads; his legs seemed fine too. "I hope it's nothing serious," worried Ace.

John nodded. "Let's ask George to look him over," he suggested.

But Christian did not seem to want to be away from Boy for very long: after a minute or two he pulled away and ran back to the enclosure, again moving perfectly normally.

Boy was strolling around his enclosure now, so Christian followed, making sure he kept a good distance between them. His alert eyes never left the bigger lion. Although Boy was now allowing Christian to come near him and

Katania, the cub was still not allowed to get too close. The three of them could be together, but Christian always kept slightly behind them – with them, but not yet quite part of their pride.

Suddenly John and Ace burst out laughing. They had noticed that Christian's limp was back again and realized what was going on. Christian wasn't hurt or injured; he was simply copying the way Boy walked, even down to his limp!

CHAPTER FIFTEEN

Soon Christian was spending more time with Boy and Katania than with John and Ace. He was tougher and more confident than he had ever been.

George had decided that it would do Christian good to be separated from John and Ace for a week or so, so the two men left the camp to allow him to get used to their absence: after all, the time was fast approaching when they would not be around at all any more.

Christian soon adapted to not having John and Ace there during the day – he actually preferred playing with Katania anyway now. The two cubs would spend hours chasing around, tripping each other up and wrestling playfully. Slowly his relationship with Boy was improving too, though the adult lion was still jealous when Christian and Katania played together for long periods of time. Every so often he would charge at Christian – just to let him know who was boss.

Every day the lions would set off on their morning walk together – Christian still a little way behind the other two, but getting closer every day. One morning George decided to watch them as they left the camp. After only a couple of minutes he noticed something frightening. Christian and Boy did too.

Quite close to the camp, by the river, there was a huge rhinoceros. It had tough grey skin and a large, very sharp horn on the front of its head. Katania quickly padded off to hide from it, and even Boy, after sizing it up for a moment, kept his distance, his eyes on the animal at all times. But Christian was still inexperienced at hunting, and he wanted to prove to Boy that he was brave and strong.

As he had done with the cow when he first arrived in Kenya, Christian stalked the animal perfectly, curving round it silently. Then, suddenly, the rhino turned and caught sight of him. It snorted with rage and charged at the lion, kicking up a cloud of dust. Christian was terrified. He realized now that there was no way he could challenge this huge creature in a fight, so he turned and fled. The rhino soon gave up, much to the relief of both Christian and his friends.

Christian had learned so much over the past month, but there were many dangers to face in Africa.

★ ★ ★

Except for this one scary incident, Christian's life was happy and peaceful. He was more independent now, he and Katania were great friends, and his relationship with Boy improved every day. He didn't really *need* his human friends at all any more.

But it soon became obvious that he still *wanted* them. Having spent two weeks away from the camp, John and Ace returned very late at night. They had only been back for a minute when Christian sensed that they had returned; following the sound of their voices, he bounded over to them ecstatically. He leaped up, grunting happily and trying to lick their faces. They were tired from their travels, but as soon as they attempted to sit down or unpack, Christian made it plain that he wanted their undivided attention; he wouldn't leave them alone.

John and Ace stared at each other as the lion

clambered onto their laps. It would soon be time to leave him here with George and the rest of his pride. They were dreading it. Christian had been the focus of their lives for nearly a year now, and they adored him. Christian loved them too. He could survive out in the wild now, but could he survive without their love? And could John and Ace live without Christian?

Their final day together did indeed arrive quickly. John and Ace knew they would be too upset to say a proper goodbye, so they planned to spend one last day with Christian before slipping away early one morning when he was still asleep.

The lion seemed to sense that they were about to leave him, and on their last day the atmosphere was tense and he wasn't as playful as usual. He stayed close to his old friends, winding himself round the backs of their legs and gently nuzzling them. As night started to fall, he led them over to the river that ran round the outside of the camp. His head was down, and he kept turning round to check that they were still behind him.

When they reached the riverbank, John and Ace sat down, and Christian snuggled in between them, nuzzling his head against their legs from time to time. Occasionally he would give a soft little grunt, but otherwise the three of them were silent.

Christian stared out at the beautiful red sunset in front of him. He blended into his surroundings perfectly. He was heavier than when he'd first arrived in Africa, and soon he'd be as tall as Boy. His tawny coat had changed again too: it was shorter and smoother, making him look more athletic. The only sign of the cub that John and Ace had taken from the cage in Harrods now were his paws. They still seemed too big for his body. If the rest of him ever matched them in size, he would truly be a huge, magnificent lion.

But he was beautiful now, and he was ready for his new life as a free lion.

John and Ace looked down proudly at the remarkable animal between them. They couldn't imagine how boring life would be without Christian. But as the three friends sat there together for the last time, they all seemed to be thinking exactly the same thing: what a wonderful year it had been for them all.

One year later, Christian padded softly out of the African wilderness into the clearing where he liked to doze under a bush when the African sun got too hot. He stopped, suddenly hearing George's voice, and went over to greet his friend.

George often came to see how Christian and the other lions were doing, but today the lion could hear other voices as well; he could smell other scents too – voices and smells he knew well.

He bounded out of the clearing towards them—he wanted to find these people quickly.

Suddenly he caught sight of them. They had spotted him as well, and they were standing smiling at him. One of the men was thinner and taller, with blond hair; the other was dark, with a happy face. They waited patiently. Christian was sure that he knew these people – finally John and Ace were back!

George had told them that now, a year on, the lion loved his new life in Africa: he had his own pride now, and he behaved exactly like a wild animal – as if he had lived in Africa all his life.

But Christian bounded over to the men in delight, throwing himself at Ace, who was closer. It was as though no time had passed since they had last seen each other. Christian placed his paws on Ace's chest and nuzzled his head and licked his face. He did the same to John. Then he ran round them happily, taking in their smell again. Every so often he would jump at them, hugging them and winding round the backs of their legs.

John and Ace had tears of happiness in their eyes.

"I can't believe it!" whispered Ace.

John shook his head. "I knew he wouldn't forget us. I just knew it."

Of course Christian hadn't forgotten John and Ace. They had taken him out of the tiny cramped cage in Harrods; they had loved him and cared for him; and they had given him this amazing chance to live as he should in Africa. Christian loved them and would never forget them. And now he wanted to introduce his friends to the rest of his pride . . .

MORE ABOUT CHRISTIAN . . .

More About Christian and His Fellow Lions . . .

Christian was born in a zoo – Ilfracombe Zoo in Devon. This zoo no longer exists, but there are lions in zoos all over the world. Outside zoos, lions can only be found in Africa and in one park in northwest India.

Adult male lions – like Christian's father, Butch, and Boy – can grow to almost 10 feet long and weigh more than 500 pounds! Lionesses like Christian's mother, Mary, can be over 8 feet long and weigh almost 300 pounds.

When Christian was first born, he, like all newborn lion cubs, was blind! Cubs' eyes only open after about two or three weeks, and it is then another week before they start seeing properly. Once the eyes are open, though, lions' vision is amazing – they can see five times better than humans.

• • • • •

In the story we see Christian rubbing heads to introduce himself to new friends. Boy and girl lions in the wild will always do this. It is so that one lion leaves its smell on the other lion as a sign of friendship and bonding.

Lions' claws are very sharp, as we see when Christian and his naughty sister cause damage to the carpets in Harrods. This is because they grow in layers: as soon as the top layer has worn down a little, it falls off and a sharp new claw is exposed. A grown-up lion's claw can be nearly 1.6 inches long.

Christian grows a mane. This is something only male lions have, and it circles their whole head and grows onto their shoulders. The hair is stiff and wiry and is different in colour from the rest of the lion's body. The mane gets bigger and darker with age.

Lions have very big appetites! In the wild their diet consists mainly of meat, and they will normally eat about 40 pounds in one go. Some can even eat up to 75 pounds! Afterwards they like to sleep for a long time – sometimes for a whole day!

Though we see Christian attempt to hunt an African cow and a rhino, in the wild the initial stalking and attack are usually the duty of the females.

• • • • •

Lions work as a team to hunt and kill animals such as antelopes, zebras and wildebeest for their family to feed on.

While the females are hunting, males often defend the pride's home, which is usually in grassland, scrub or open woodland. They mark it out as their territory by urinating around it!

Lions are the only animals in the cat family that live in groups. These groups are called prides. Prides usually include three or four males, between four and twenty females, and all their cubs. Females mostly stay with the same pride for their whole life.

Once a male lion is between two and three years old, he is usually chased out of his pride and must try to establish his own.

Boy tries to teach Christian to respect him. All cubs must respect their elders. When a lioness brings home the food she has caught, cubs only get some once all the adults have had their fill.

When Christian moves to Africa, he gets thorns caught in the soft pads of his paws. These pads enable lions to move quietly so that the animals they are hunting won't hear them coming.

• • • • •

Only four big cats can roar – lions, tigers, leopards and jaguars – and of these, the lion roars the most. A lion's roar can be heard about five miles away!

Christian struggles to get used to the heat in Kenya. Lots of lions do, and because of this they tend to hunt at night or early in the morning, when it is slightly cooler.

Christian is left on his own in Kenya when he is just over one year old. However, lions don't reach their full size or have their full manes until they are about five. Lions reach old age when they are between ten and fifteen years old.

Although lions grow very big, they can still move

quickly when they want to – they can reach speeds of up to 50 miles an hour for a short time. They can also leap more than 30 feet.

Very sadly, the number of lions in the world is decreasing all the time. We can never get an exact number of how many there are, but it is thought that there are fewer than 30,000 African lions in the wild now.

Dotty Rhino and the George Adamson Wildlife Preservation Trust

ALL ABOUT THE TRUST

Dotty Rhino is part of the George Adamson Trust, which was founded in 1980 by a group of George's friends. It is based in Mkomazi, which is in Tanzania, very close to Kenya, where Christian was released into the wild.

It is now run by Tony Fitzjohn (Fitz), who worked with George for many years. Together, they have released more than 30 lions just like Christian into the wild. Mkomazi now protects endangered species like black rhinos and wild dogs, making sure they are safe from poachers. Fitz and his family and 'The Crew' – 45 men and women who help him run the camp – now do amazing work in Mkomazi. They build roads, dig water holes, construct dams, fix machinery and help local villages.

ALL ABOUT GEORGE ADAMSON

George is best known for *Born Free,* the book and film based on his real-life experiences raising Elsa, his adopted lion cub, with his wife, Joy.

He was born in India in 1906 and first visited Kenya in 1924. He joined Kenya's game department in 1937, and six years later married Joy. It was in 1956 that he met Elsa, the cub that would become famous in *Born Free.*

In 1970 George moved to Kora in northern Kenya to rehabilitate Christian and all the other lions in the man-made pride he had assembled.

He died in 1989, aged 83.

HOW YOU CAN GET INVOLVED

Dotty Rhino's aims are to raise awareness, to educate and to support the George Adamson Wildlife Preservation Trust.

Visit the website at www.dottyrhino.com for more information, details on how you can help, fun stuff, games and much more!

ELSA

Elsa is a real-life lion that became famous through the book and film *Born Free*. After their mother died, she and her two sisters, Big One and Lustica, were taken in by George and Joy Adamson. Her sisters were sent to live in a zoo, but Elsa stayed with the Adamsons and was very happy there.

Joy and George taught Elsa all the skills she needed to survive on her own in the wild. After her release, when she was three years old, she brought three of her own cubs to show them. Very sadly, Elsa died from a blood disease not long after, but her story lives on in *Born Free*.

ASLAN

Aslan is the central character in *The Chronicles of Narnia* by C. S. Lewis, and he is the only character to appear in all seven books in the series. There have been lots of portrayals of Aslan in the various television and screen adaptations of the books, and many famous actors have provided Aslan's voice, including Liam Neeson and David Suchet.

In the stories, Aslan is shown as wise and loving, and he guides and protects all the human children who visit Narnia. His name, Aslan, is the Turkish word for *lion*.

THE COWARDLY LION

The Cowardly Lion is one of the main characters in *The Wonderful Wizard of Oz,* by L. Frank Baum, and the film *The Wizard of Oz,* starring Judy Garland.

Lions are thought of as brave and powerful, the King of Beasts, so the Cowardly Lion thinks that his constant fear makes him inadequate. He travels with Dorothy along the Yellow Brick Road to ask the Wizard for some courage. But along the way he learns that courage is more than just roaring at people.

Some Fascinating Facts About Christian's New Home ...

KENYA FACT FILE

Capital: Nairobi.

Time: GMT +3 hours.

Distance from UK: nearly 4,000 miles.

Population: approximately 27 million.

First language: Swahili.

Local currency: Kenyan shilling.

Country motto: 'Let us all pull together.'

Climate: The weather in Kenya can be unpredictable and tends to vary in different regions, but it is typically hot and sunny throughout most of the year.

Highest mountain: Mount Kenya (17,057 feet).

Wildlife: All the big five animals of Africa can be found living wild in Kenya. The big five are: lions, elephants, buffalo, leopards and rhinos.

AFRICAN ELEPHANT FACT FILE

Male: Bull.

Female: Cow.

Types of elephant: The African and the Asian; the African elephant is the larger of the two.

Average height: 11.94 feet at the shoulder (male), 9.84 feet (female).

Average weight: 12,026 pounds (male), 8,016 pounds (female).

Life expectancy: Elephants can live to the age of 70 or more.

Behaviour: Amazingly, elephants can cry, play and laugh! They also grieve when one of their number dies.

Tusks: Elephant tusks are actually teeth and can be amost 8 feet long. Elephants use them to dig up roots and to fight.

AFRICAN BUFFALO FACT FILE
(also known as Cape buffalo)

Average size: 5.58 feet high, 11.15 feet long.

Average weight: 1,450 pounds.

Appearance: Coat is dark brown in colour; they are a member of the cow family and have large curved horns.

Habitat: Swamps, floodplains, forests and grasslands.

Diet: African buffalo are herbivores and eat coarse grass.

Predators: Lions, crocodiles, leopards and spotted hyenas.

Behaviour: The African buffalo is a herd animal, undomesticated and dangerous to humans. African buffalo are thought to vote on which direction the herd should take.

LEOPARD FACT FILE

Places where leopards are found: Africa, Asia.

Average size: 2.95 to 6.23 feet long.

Average weight: Up to 200 pounds –
they are the fifth largest feline in the world.

Attributes: Graceful, stealthy, agile; leopards
are good stalkers and great swimmers.

Leopard family: Includes panthers and black jaguars.

Habitat: Savannahs, jungles, mountains and forests.

Diet: Monkeys, antelopes, wildebeests,
snakes, sheep, goats and insects.

Only predator: Humans!

Interesting fact: Leopards can drag something
three times their own weight up into trees!

BLACK RHINO FACT FILE

Colour: The black rhino is in fact grey!

Conservation status: Severely endangered.

Found in: Eastern and southern Africa.

Habitat: Grassland, wooded savannah.

Diet: Herbivores.

Average weight: 1,764 to 2,976 pounds.

Life expectancy: Up to 50 years.

Attributes: Bad eyesight, good hearing and fantastic sense of smell. The black rhino can be very aggressive.

Only predators: Humans!

Interesting facts: Black rhinos love taking baths – mud baths! They can go for up to five days without drinking any water! And their top speed is 36 miles per hour!

ANTHONY "ACE" BOURKE

was born in Sydney in 1946. He has become one of Australia's leading art curators, a pioneer in the field of Aboriginal art, and a colonial art specialist, staging numerous critically acclaimed exhibitions. Ace hopes to immerse himself again in wildlife and conservation projects, to help address the world's urgent environmental issues. He lives in Sydney with his two cats.

JOHN RENDALL

is a sixth-generation Australian and divides his time between London and Sydney. He continues his commitment to the George Adamson Wildlife Preservation Trust and is a member of the Royal Geographical Society in London. He has been involved in travel-focused public relations, concentrating on conservation projects, lodges, and reserves in Africa. John's three children share his passion for wildlife and conservation.